Sex, Relationships, and Sometimes... Love

A MONOLOGUES SHOW

WRITTEN BY Joelle Arqueros

authorHOUSE®

AuthorHouse™
1663 Liberty Drive, Suite 200
Bloomington, IN 47403
www.authorhouse.com
Phone: 1-800-839-8640

First published by AuthorHouse 10/28/2008

ISBN: 978-1-4343-6988-8 (sc)

Printed in the United States of America
Bloomington, Indiana

This book is printed on acid-free paper.

For

Ben,
Baby Ben,
Bernie,
and of course,
Bukowski's BlueBird

Original cast of
Sex, Relationships, and Sometimes...Love
at "Show World" on 9th Ave. and 44th St. 2003

Directed and Produced by Joelle Arqueros

Carolyn Campisi

April Allen

Ailene Quinlan

Joseph Geller

Rob Ringley

Michael Leach

France – Luce Benson

Joel Roman

Jon Sebastian

Isis

Michael Harmon

Erinrose Widner

Cindy Marinangel

Original cast at
The Complex, Sierra Stages and The Actor's Playpen
in Hollywood California 2004

Written and Directed by Joelle Arqueros
Produced by Nicolas Read

Lavonne

Naidra Dawn Thomson

Elizabeth Magness

Sarah Andrews

Nicolas Read

Jazzmun

Robert Burnett

Kelsea Button

Luoc Lee

Eric Erickson

Skye Passmore

Sam Hargrave

Brian Dembkowski

Terri Shusta

Dawn Meyer

Audrey Sarn

Holly Beavon

Shoobie

Ryuma Hyrano

Joshua Grant

Darwin Harris

Sufe Bradshaw

Jimmy Lyons

Skye Passmore

Joanna Houghton

Lindsay Dane

Robert Morgan

Mari Marks

Leslie Intriago

Tiffinany Alden

Sarah Bogatti

Brian Barth

Kristan Cleto

Donna Letterese

Jonathan Garcia

Justin Marchert

Michelle Mellgren

CONTENTS

♀ *usually* done by female

♂ *usually* done by male

☿ *usually* done by male or female or other

Blue Light Special

Did you know that the first time I saw a penis was at K-mart? Yeah, my mother had taken me and my brother there to buy some shoes. She made me watch the wagon in the little girl's section while she took my brother over to the little boy's section. I remember how excited I was when I noticed that somehow a pair of ladies high heels had gotten in with the little girl's shoes and I grabbed them immediately and tried them on, looking in the mirror, pretending I was Cinderella! I didn't notice that some man was coming over towards me. He had on these really short, red silky shorts, a shirt with the sleeves cut off, and mirrored sunglasses, when I finally did notice him. For some reason I was drawn to him, but I don't really know why. I guess it was just because there was no one else around. I remember he stopped and slid his hand down a pair of little girl's pants that were hanging on a rack as he kneeled down in front of me. Then I saw it. I was instantly terrified, but I didn't really know why... It was just so... ugly. I looked at his eyes, and even though he had on those mirrored sunglasses, I could still see his eyes looking at me... waiting. So... I began to cry, and... that made him... smile.

Then he got up and walked away. My hands were trembling as I took those heels off so fast. They were EVIL... But you know what? *(beat)* Now I wear them all the fucking time.

NOTES

NOTES

Friendly Fire

She invited me to dinner. She said she wanted to talk. She had me by the balls, this girl. I found myself preparing for our encounter the entire day. I really wanted her back, and I couldn't deny it to myself any longer. Damn it, I still loved her... with every bit of me. So... I bought a new shirt, I washed my car. I even got one of those patches you put on your nose and then rip off. My nose felt really clean... and I was feeling like a real Casanova. She... looked like an angel as she came running towards me smiling. And all I could think was... I want her back, I want her back, I want her back! She looked at me... and sighed because... she knew. She could always see right through me. I loved her because of it. And... I hated her because of it. I couldn't speak throughout most of the dinner, neither could she... until we ordered a piece of cheesecake like we always did. But before our first bite she told me that she just knew I wasn't "the one" AND that I was never going to be "the one". I felt like nothing would ever taste sweet to me again! I wanted to knock her out and return the blow that she had just given me. I wanted to stop time right then and there so our dinner would never end and she could never leave me. I wanted her to stay right there in front of me until I convinced her that she could absolutely not live without me. We were so close to having something and it hurt more to get a glimpse of what that feels like... and then just have it ripped away. But... then I realized... this dinner wasn't the start at all... it was really the end. And I watched her leave me... her beautiful presence walked out of that restaurant leaving me there watching her disappear... So, I sat there... alone, drank my Heinekens... and went home... with the waitress.

NOTES

NOTES

ALLY

Yesterday I found out that my friend Ally, who I grew up with, is dead. She was found naked in the Hollywood Hills. Her mother said that the police think she was strangled, but they couldn't be sure because her body hadn't been discovered for about eight days. What happened to you, Ally? Where are you girl?

Ally and I used to hitchhike all over Hollywood. She was the only girl I knew who wanted to ditch school and down a bottle of Black Velvet Whiskey at age sixteen. I remember the time she asked me to come with her to get an abortion. She was two-and-a-half months pregnant and just wanted to "get rid of it." I'll never understand how *or why* she wanted to do it without any anesthesia. But she absolutely refused. She said that she could … handle the pain. "Handle the pain." I wonder what would've happened if she had kept that baby in her body. Would she be alive today? Would the baby have given her a reason to get her life together? Or at least we'd have a *piece* of her alive. But now it's like she's all gone … like she's *vanished*. I feel certain that if I went right now and drove down the Hollywood Hills where we used to party every weekend that I'd be able to hear her laughing … or complaining about someone taking too big of a hit off her weed.

After I finally got an apartment with two other girls, Ally moved into the living room for a month. We went shopping one day and I remember how much I loved driving her around in my beat-up old Mustang. To us, it was a Mercedes. Well, on this particular day, we bought guacamole and Boone's Strawberry Hill wine, brought it home and set it all up with tortilla chips and lit candles everywhere. It was a cold, rainy day, but we were inside together … and warm … and just as Ally was about to light up one of her famous blunts, we heard the front door start to open, which meant we would have to share our feasts with my two roommates! So we both looked at each other with our eyes opened wide and instantly started grabbing everything, trying to move it all into my room within ten seconds of a key opening a door, and the *fear* of getting caught in this silly, selfish act made us both howl with ticklish laughter. I will never forget that rainy day, and that memory will help me keep Ally alive.

We made out with boys together in the upstairs sections of the auditorium, and we shared a toothbrush on more than one occasion. Ally had golden brown hair, and a widow's peak hairline like Marilyn Monroe. She had full lips, a sexy walk, and … she loved to get high. It's crazy to think that if I still lived in Hollywood, and never moved to New York … if I had just kept an eye on her, maybe she could be *here* … *with me*, right now. But then again, it's also possible … that I could be with her.

NOTES

NOTES

Bulgarian Princess

Last night I went to dinner with my boyfriend and his older brother's girlfriend. It was her birthday and her whole family had flown in from Bulgaria to be with her on this "joyous occasion." Her father was a big burly man with a sweet glitter in his eye every time he looked at his daughter, who was obviously his diamond, his princess, his... whatever, you get the picture. And well, it was nice to see a daddy adore his daughter so much, and in a very non-sexual way, I might add. By the time the entrees came, he was... rubbing her cheeks, and stroking her arms... AND Then... he looked lovingly into her eyes and told her that he would Never... Ever... miss one birthday, no matter where he was. He promised.

Well that was about all I could take. I've never had a father. He left my mother a little after I was born, and he's missed not only every one of my birthdays but my entire life. I mean, I did have an alcoholic stepfather for a couple of months here and there, and he had a sweet glitter in his eye every time he saw a bottle of Smirnoff vodka. But even he eventually left for good too. So, without trying to be bitter, I mean really battling to not indulge in jealously, and become the all-too-easy bitter bitch, I found myself staring at this Bulgarian young woman, younger than I am, and asking... as I drank MY Smirnoff vodka martini straight-up... why the fuck do you get a daddy who loves you and I don't? How did you become so perfect and so normal, and what the fuck did I do wrong? Why wasn't I allowed love from a man who never wanted to sleep with me, unconditionally, adoringly? Why am I punished? Why? What did I do?

But... then my boyfriend looked at me for a moment... he could hear my thoughts... he touched by wrist and then asked me if I wanted the last strawberry from his plate... by the time I swallowed it, SOMEHOW my fake smile turned sincere at this beautiful young woman. And I dug deep, deep inside myself until I was happy that at least she had been blessed by something so wonderful... And I tried to love her... and not hate her... and it worked. (*beat*) It worked.

NOTES

NOTES

Someone

Ok so here it is: my name is Audrey and I'm a lesbian. Wait wait... Not only am a lesbian but I'm a JEWISH lesbian. Wait wait... Not only am I a Jewish lesbian but I have breast cancer... and I... could -possibly- die. But as bad all that may sound, it is sooooooo much better than not knowing. No one could figure out what was wrong with me. Every doctor sent me to another. It was like growing up all over again when my mother and father couldn't figure out what was wrong with me. Just why, they wanted to know, did I refuse to go out with all the nice Jewish boys who were on their way to becoming doctors and lawyers? "What's wrong with you Deborah, such a pretty girl, a shana punim' what's wrong with Shlomo? Can't you at least give him a chance? Or what about Ari, he's such a nice boy and from such a nice family." I did everything else right, I went to Hebrew school on Sundays, I had my Bad Mitzvah, I loved my religion and did very well in school, had lots of girlfriends and I mean girl FRIENDS. But when it came to boys... I found that I preferred the company of the only two boys in my Home Economics class, Fernando and Hugh. This dynamic duo took me out of Brooklyn and showed me another side of life... MANHATTAN. Oh boy oh boy oh boy, party party party. I remember one night, in the middle of the west village I saw them kiss each other. And I do not mean a Shabbat Shalom kiss on the cheek that you give to your cousin, I mean a real boy on boy, tongues and all, French kiss. I freaked out and started laughing. I thought it was a joke and they were just trying to shock me, but... then they didn't stop... and seemed to forget that I was even there. And can I just tell you... that was the first time I ever felt so aroused in my nineteen years of life. What they did for me, no Shlomo could ever do. And I guess I KNEW that... before I actually KNEW that. This new exciting life of loving whom you love instead of loving whom you were supposed to love, it fed me, freedom, strength, and... independence as an individual. That very night enlightened me and gave me a courage I never knew I had. Unfortunately... it wasn't enough courage for Corrina. Corrina was an Italian girl from a family who hated Blacks, Puerto Ricans, Jews and especially... "the queers." And I loved her the minute I laid my eyes on her black long hair, green eyes and red lips. We both worked as hostesses at a restaurant at Kings Plaza in Brooklyn and became very close. We would go to the movies together and parties. One night, I remember a couple of gay men left the restaurant and all of the male waiters began whistling and cat calling... One guy even actually spit at them! Corrina whispered to me that she felt "so sorry for them, the queers, they were so sick in the head and should get help from a psychiatrist or mental institution." I was appalled but knew she had spent her life being brain washed. But then a few days later we were at her house, lying on the floor, looking through Vogue or Cosmo -she had tons of those girly magazines- when Corrina said (beat) that she had decided to stop liking her favorite supermodel because she had read that this Supermodel was a lesbian. Well I couldn't stand her existing like this anymore so I lied to her and told her that I had kissed a girl before - even though I hadn't. She told me to stop lying but I insisted I had. Somehow we dropped it but wouldn't you know it, the very next time we got drunk together... she asked me to kiss her! What was I suppose to do? Tell her that I lied? At that very moment I felt that the gay community was relying on me to represent. I wanted her to open her mind and be able to grow... she deserved more... So... I took a deep breath and kissed her with all of the sparkling erotica that embodied my little Jewish heart and soul... And man did she respond the most fiery Italian tomato sauces that I had ever tasted... and... am I grateful to her ancestors. Well, need I say that was just the first course and dessert lasted for the next 3 years. Everyone assumed we were just best friends. Girls can get away with that with slumber parties and what not. It was a dream, it was heaven, it was love in all that love should ever hope to be until... MARCELLO PRESIOZO started to work for Corrina's father and Corrina's father decided it was time for Corrina to get married. She new it was unbearable for me to be around them and I slowly saw her less and less. I had to accept it. I knew she would never have the strength to go against her father. So she said that every time I was with her and Marcello, she would sing: "There's a somebody I'm longing to see," and I would know that that somebody was me and that she truly loved me and wished that it was just the two of us. We cried the entire night before her wedding... I was the maid of honor! I bawled throughout the entire ceremony. Everyone kept saying, "Oh how sweet is Audrey? So happy for her friend." They had no clue I was deciding the easiest way to kill him and, if I could somehow, put my name on his ticket to Mexico for the honeymoon. Well I didn't kill him and they drove away from the church in a Cadillac with cans dangling from the back that I spent hours attaching. And I never spoke to her again until... yesterday morning. She heard I was sick and wanted to see me... but... I waited all day... all night... she never showed. I understand... it's been a very long time , I'd heard she'd had at least two babies. I bet they are beautiful. So beautiful. Corrina... I pray she's happy... but not too happy. Between you and I... out of all of my life's romances, I'm still waiting for Corrina to come back from Mexico and tell me she can't live without me because, (sings) "There's a somebody I'm longing to see..

NOTES

NOTES

You #1

I love you so much that you may be the only man inside of me ever again. Do you know what that means?! I never thought I could get so much satisfaction from just one man... but now that I have met YOU... I KNOW that I can! EVERY time I look at you, I am actually looking... into the face of the MAN... that I have been WAITING for, and SEARCHING for, my whole life! I can't believe it! You are... "it." And "it" is like... a miracle and everything is fitting so perfectly and feeling so right on... and our lovemaking is actually LOVE-MAKING. I don't think I have ever done that before! It is better and better every time, and when I go to sleep... I wake up loving you more and more. It is like we have been blessed and I am so so scared that maybe someday it will end and I will feel so empty inside. BUT SOMEhow I have the courage to accept this possibility and still move forward with you. YES! I can't imagine existing ever again without your presence near to me... I miss you when you are in the shower, or going down to throw out he trash, or moving the car... I am loveSICK and I can only pray that I am never... ever... cured.

NOTES

You #2

I HATE you so much… that you may be the only man alive who I truly wish were dead! Everytime I think of you… I can't believe that I actually fell for all of your stupid, conniving, manipulations. You are worth nothing, do you here me? A mere piece of nothing. It is like I have been cursed by your existence on this earth and the world would be so gracious and cleansed if you were just gone, never born, erased! I feel like I need to spend my life in the shower just to wash you away from me. I have to MOVE to remove myself from any toxic breathe of yours that may linger in my house! I am loveSICK and I can only pray… that when I tell your… wife… YOU will never… ever… be cured.

NOTES

Awakenings

I was supposed to ask her to marry me. I was her faithful, loving boyfriend for two years. I was everything I was suppose to be. I was faithful, sensitive, generous… encouraging. The only thing I wasn't… was… straight. I just wasn't… and let me tell you I tried to be. I tried to "make" myself feel attracted to her. After all, she WAS beautiful. But he… he was more beautiful, at least to me. I kept thinking maybe if I'd never taken that flight or maybe if I had slept through the peanuts and the drinks, maybe then I would have never met Brett and never even known that I was gay. God… I can't believe I actually thought that. Well, Melissa was the one who slept and as soon as I felt Brett's hand, as he served me my Bloody Mary, I knew. I knew. Like the answer to a question that had been festering so deep inside me that I never even allowed myself to hear… until just then. That day. In the sky… on my way to a romantic suite in Acapulco with Melissa… a ring in my pocket! He knew it too. We talked together in the back of the plane for the rest of the flight. And he asked me for my number and told me that he just had to see me again. And… when he kissed me on the mouth I felt more… AWAKE… then

I had ever felt before in my life. I could hardly make it back to my seat, my knees were shaking… and Melissa, Melissa, what was I going to tell Melissa? She was the one I told everything to. What did all of this really even mean? Just what was I getting myself into? And as I watched her sleeping so sweetly I felt… evil. Evil and dangerous. I hardly knew myself. What I did know was that I wasn't going to be asking Melissa to marry me. And I finally knew why I'd been putting it off for so long. See… the truth was I really did love Melissa and I couldn't go on lying to her or to myself.

That was four years ago. Brett and I are still together and in love. Melissa married a nice guy named Frank… he works in a bank. I never got an invitation. I persistently told her that it wasn't her fault. That she didn't "turn me gay," that was impossible. It really had nothing to do with her. But I know her. She will always assume that she did something wrong to make me leave her for a man. But that's not true, the only man I left her for was… me.

NOTES

NOTES

I Can't Get No...

He was this big!! (*holding up her hands seven inches apart*) And he was only twenty-two! But what good is this (*showing seven inches again*), when he finishes so quickly I can't put it to good use anyhow? I mean, at first I was like "Okay, so he can't please me every time." But then it just kept happening, ya know, over and over and over until I became so enraged with utter... frustration... that I just BLURTED out, "IF THIS HAPPENS ONE MORE TIME YOU'D BETTER GET ONE OF YOUR FRIENDS OVER TO FINISH THE JOB FOR YOU !!!"

And he got upset? I mean, WHY is it... that when THEY finish first, it is over, out of service, but for the one or two times that WE actually finish first... we are OBLIGATED to keep going AND to pretend like we are still in to it? I mean shouldn¹t they feel obligated to keep going? Oh yeah... TRY mentioning that... and all you get is... "I AM NOT A MACHINE!!!" So, we finally decided to compromise... we decided that every time he felt like he was gonna' finish first... I would just... slap him across the face... you know, to break up the mood a little, and well... at first I was a little uncomfortable... and I was like, (*demonstrating with her hand, timidly*) slap, slap. But then I really started getting into it and I was like SLAP! SLAP! SLAP!!! Until... he started CRYING!! Confesses that he is only seventeen!!! Pulls a fucking SKATEBOARD out of his gym bag and skates off! Leaving me there, watching from the window, thinking to myself,... "CALL ME." Well at least I am not dating that med student anymore WE never had time for romance... and when he finally did decide to squeeze in a little sex, he would get on top of me like a jackhammer, then pull up his pants and say, "I HAVE TO GO STUDY!!! I HAVE TO GO STUDY!" Leaving me there, covered in his chest hair, sizzling like a hot fucking fajita platter! Soooo... I finally decided to confide in my husband Jack... I said, "Jack, honey, it would really please me...no no no ... Damn it Jack, it has always been a fantasy of mine... to be in the middle of taking a hot shower... when the shower curtain is suddenly ripped open by a stranger in a black ski mask with a gun, or... or... a knife in his hand... and he grabs me out of the shower and throws me down on the bed dripping wet! So... one day I am in the shower, and I'm lathering up all good and soapy, when I hear someone come into the bathroom... and the shower curtain is ripped open! And there is Jack...WITH A SCUBA MASK, A SNORKLE, AND A G-D DAMN PLUNGER IN HIS HAND!!! I give up.

NOTES

NOTES

I Promise

Can I tell you something? Last night I dreamt that I gave birth to a baby... and... when I looked in his eyes he had the most beautiful green eyes, and I could see MY eyes when I looked in his. I said... "Hi." and he said "Hi." back to me and smiled. Now, I know it may sound crazy to think of a newborn baby saying "Hi." but I heard it, and perhaps only I could... like a special voice that only a momma can hear. And I loved him more than the love I've always known to be the greatest love... This love was energizing, and awakening to my soul. I felt that my arms would mold heavenly to his glorious little being and I felt... happy and in love with life for allowing a human to experience this overwhelming feeling of nerves warmed with a glowing gratefulness to be able to truly see the meaning of existence! But... then ... I woke up. And I was thirty-two without a boyfriend... When can we meet again in reality? Where is daddy? Don't worry my son... I'll find him... I promise.

NOTES

My Mission

So she tells me that she just wants to let me know that I shouldn't like her, that I should INSTEAD like one of her friends because... she's not gonna' put out... at all... in any way whatsoever not even a kiss! (*beat*) She says she doesn't want me to "waste my time" even talking to her. Now I can look at this in two ways:

One: just who the hell do you think you are? Assuming... I even WANT to sleep with you, you conceited delusional bitch, you should be so lucky to get anywhere near my manliness, -or-

Two: damn this girl is mad cool saving me a lot of time with this inside scoop of information so that I can continue on my mission.

However... BECAUSE she has given me this information... my mission... has become unclear... I am suddenly... distracted... and NEED to know WHY? WHY? WHY? Why DOESN'T she want to sleep with me not even kiss me?? Have I... turned her off in some way? Am I... not her type? Just WHAT is it about

ME that let's her know IMMEDIATELY that she does not want me?! Or... or... or is she just SAYING all of this so that I will fight for her? Hmmm... So I tell her, (*clearing his throat, fixing his hair etc.*) "Listen... I don't want your FRIENDS... I want YOU... and I will be PERFECTLY satisfied just TALKING to you." She smiles... and I just know that I am gonna' get some eventually! The mission begins!

NOTES

NOTES

Ever After

Now as a Hispanic male I seem to automatically get a bad rap. I'm serious. Women always assume I'm a player, playboy, womanizer, liar... I mean come on, don't judge me ladies. Yes I admit that Latin men are known to have many offspring and by many different ladies, perhaps. But that does not mean that we are all this way. Do not assume that I am incapable of devoting myself to one woman. As a matter of a fact I am in love with one woman as I speak. Madly in love. She is my wife and we have been married over two and a half years now. But you know what? She's cheating on me, yo. And it's not like I did something terrible. Or we had a big fight. Honestly, no. It's not like there is a rule I didn't follow or a way I neglected her. I always remember the little things and all that. I enjoy considering her when I make decision... no nothing like that really. One day she just came home and she looked at me differently it was like... she was kidnapped from right inside her body. And you know what? I love her so much that I am afraid to even mention it. There is something in my heart telling me she might actually leave me for him if she finds out that I am aware. So I watch her get ready to leave and I know the days when she sees him because there's something extra. You know when she gets out of the shower, when she dresses, when she combs her hair, there is an urgency, an excitement in her energy and I can sense it. It screams at me silently. I can tap into it so quickly and so easily because I remember it... it use to happen so often when she looked at me. I wonder why I still feel it for her. I am amazed by the way I can't stop loving her, wanting her. It's almost admirable... almost. But then she says goodbye, like a wife and smiles without looking in my eyes, and the door shuts and she's gone. The house is silent and I am consumed by fear. Fear that she won't come home... fear that she will.

NOTES

NOTES

Sumi's Hands

I remember the first time I kissed a girl I was seventeen and a half and in Japan. I had been dating Sumi for a little over two months. She was the boss's daughter and had a very cute face. I remember after I kissed her, she looked deeply onto my eyes and told me that I was a terrible kisser. I couldn't believe that I waited two months and this was her response! I decided that I would learn how to kiss better and started watching a lot of Japanese soap operas... especially one called, "MY SISTER WAS WATCHING" which had a lot of long, deep kisses. I think it helped! Because she actually seemed to be enjoying my kisses after a while! And we held hands... whenever we were alone.

Two years later I moved to America and began working in another restaurant. I also began dating an American girl who was ten years older than I am. On our first date, she took me to the beach and began kissing and touching me all over the sand! She was the very opposite of Sumi and very, very aggressive. She took me to her house and we had sex on the first date. It was my first time and I was incredibly nervous but she completely took

over and… we… we began doing it often. But before I knew it…
she began taking over my life! And insisted that I start going
to church. She also wanted to know where I was every second
of the day. She also insisted that I have no female friends, or
doctors or dentists! If we went to the grocery store, I had to
pick a line where the check out clerk was MALE! I was really
enjoying her seduction, but she was beginning to drive me crazy
so I decided to break it off and I haven't had sex since! I miss
her sex… but most of all, I really miss is Sumi, and holding her
hands whenever we were alone.

NOTES

NOTES

Weening

Females? Oh well sure of course I've had females in my life.
But they just cannot seem to compete with, well... MOTHER.
(*sighs*) MOTHER. She truly is the number one female in my
life. THE STAR! She is always there for me, MOTHER,
doing the cooking, and the cleaning, the laundry. She even
irons my underwear! It feels so good to put on a clean pair of
iron warmed tightie whities... AND NO CREASES! If I am
ever feeling sad or lonely MOTHER will drop everything and
spend the night with me! Our special sleepovers. She talks to
me about my troubles until I fall asleep on her bosom and then
in he morning she makes me chocolate chip pancakes shaped just
like little bears! Oh yeah, oh yeah, I know what your thinking,
I know what your thinking. I am a grown man, right? What
about sex? Don't I have desires? Of course! AND Mother is
right on top of that one too! Do you know that she loves me
so much that she brought me a catalogue full of pictures of
beautiful young females making all kinds of gymnastic type
poses in their underwear? She allows me to pick one out all by
myself -respecting my independence like she always does- and

then... sends the female to bounce on me... after she is screened by our family doctor of course. Then mother will wait in her car across the street patiently -respecting my privacy- usually no longer than six minutes or so will pass when I walkie talkie her... to let her know I have finished so she can pay the bill and draw me a hot bubble bath, reminding me to scrub my pee pee spic and span. (*Sighs*) I love mother. I get a different female every week! Mother doesn't think it's healthy to have the same female more than once. I've tried to date women that I meet at work or at church. But the dates haven't been so successful. One woman was actually offended when MOTHER showed up at dinner to put on my bib. -We were eating pasta with red sauce... I could have ruined my shirt! It is just so sad... females today, they just can't seem to accept a man who is close to his... Mother.

NOTES

NOTES

Morning Sun

Whenever the morning sun would come in the window, I would always wake up and the first thing I'd go see was it shining and dancing and glowing in her long baby girl hair. Long and beautiful. I loved to touch it and pet it and even pull it gently at times. She was my beautiful, little, golden princess and I loved her. I did love her. And I don't care what no policeman, judge, detective, forensic asshole says. I love her. I do. And not even her own mama can tell me any different. After all she is our little girl, why shouldn't I love her? She loves me too, I know she does. I can still remember the first day we kissed deeply on the mouth. She had those wide eyes staring at me like "Daddy what is this?" I knew then that I could teach her so much. And I felt it was my place to. Not some stranger, some high school boy or football hero lying to her. Let's face it, Daddy knows best. When she was with me I was always gentle. She was always safe with daddy. My beautiful baby girl. I will be out of here soon. And we can be together and in love again and I can watch the sun dancing in your hair again. Dancing so pretty. I'll watch it making you glow and light up in my eyes. They can't keep us apart forever. They can't. I won't let them.

NOTES

Bon Appetit

Just listen now honey and stop crying. He is not worth your tears, baby. NO MAN IS, and that is why... I am gonna' let you in on a little secret. You see sweetie, I have developed a "method" for the magnificent woman of today, and EVERYday. It is called the "Circulation Flavor Wheel." That's right, and all you have to do is pick out your favorite flavors... hmmm example? A spicy Puerto Rican lover with mocha skin and light eyes, hmmm irresistible... or maybe a macho Italian stallion with full lips reeking of cologne, mmm delicious... or how about a chiseled, dark chocolate black man with strong arms and a beautiful pink tongue, mmmmmm. Yeah. Oh yeah, umm, what was my point? Oh yes! Whatever your taste is, CIRCULATE, yes, you see honey you have to circulate the men in your life and keep that flavor wheel spinning 'cause as soon as you allow one to stay too long, everything starts to get fucked up and out of balance. And you know it usually takes about two or three men to make up one good one anyhow! You only live once and this is a wonderful way to really discover what is on your MEN-U! So bon appetit, sister! And stop eating that same damn cheeseburger every night! What you need is a well-balanced meal that will give you the nutrients your precious little heart and soul needs. Wow, how do you like that? It seems to be time for dinner. In the mood for Chinese?*

*Suggested cuisine can be any type of food, usually relating to the performer.

NOTES

NOTES

She Can't
Be Trusted

Hi, how ya' doin'? Yeah well, uh, I'm having a lot of problems with my girl. Actually, our relationship is basically over, but we're at that end where we have them nightmare screaming phone conversations over and over until I wind up saying, "Fuck you, cunt!" and hang up on her. Which I guess is sort of unfair... since what can she really retaliate with after "Cunt?" ... "Dick?" That just doesn't cut like "Cunt," ya' know? Or even "Slut." I mean, I know that hurts her. But if she calls me a slut, is it really gonna' hurt me? I don't think so. However, she is a fuckin' slut. Can you believe she went back to working at one of them "Gentlemen's Clubs" again? But you know there ain't no "gentlemen" there. Everyone who steps into one of those places is a fuckin' loser. She sells cigars to these pricks while all these girls are walking around naked. We've had this problem before. This girl loves topless bars! Can you imagine? A girls who loves to watch naked women dance for her? I never heard of such a thing! She says that it's an "art" and that women are beautiful and have the right to express themselves sexually if they choose. That's what I get for going out with a girl from California... and she's not even a lesbian! Or so she says... Well, that's all right, 'cause I mean, I told her... if she wants to be with me, I'm the MAN, and I lay down the law. As long as she's my girl, she does what I say. There's no reason why I should ever see her lips moving to talk to another guy, ever! As long as she's with me: no clubs, no parties, no short skirts, no slutty friends, no working with guys, no making decisions about anything without me EVER. She got upset the other day because I didn't spend the day with her or get her anything for her birthday. Stugatz! She doesn't understand... that that's what she gets for trying to be a rebel. She wants the good things... but she doesn't want to do right. I can't be with a girl like that. She wants to come and go as she pleases. I-DON'T-THINK-SO. But you know what? One day she's gonna' wake up and she's gonna' say, "You know, Paulie? You were right."

My mother was the same way. She cheated on my father for a long time with a scumbag she worked for. The whole neighborhood knew. He used to come to my house, honking his fuckin' flashy Corvette, throwin' it all in our face. And all my father did was cry... Fuckin' coward. I almost got arrested five times for trying to kill that scumbag, while my father did nothing but ask me and my two brothers, "Why is she doing this?"

What a wimp. Well, that's never gonna' happen to me. I'll have my girl in check. No freedom so she can cheat. Not even if I love her... She can't be trusted.

NOTES

NOTES

So Bored With You

Listen… I'd seduce you but… why? I'm not really that into you. Yes I thought you were hot… but now the more that I know you, not a thing about you… motivates me. I love your eyes… and your big pouty lips… but you… you want me so badly I won't feel like I'm RAPING you at all!

AND that is so very… very… boring. AAAHHHH… what to do, what to do? I feel like listening to French music while drinking crispy cold wine, on a hot beach… at dusk… in just a lemon colored g- string… tanned from a long hot day of… running on the beach… laughing… the hot wind blowing in my hair… against my bare shoulders… my neck… my… face… my lips. I want to be in LOVE! …and pour myself all over someone, licking their delicious skin! Someone… else… not you… wont you please leave…? I'd like to be… alone.

NOTES

Fearless

I saw "him" as soon as he walked in the restaurant and he looked up at me with such an... "OPENESS" that the hair on the back of my neck stood up. He seemed... fearless! AND it was not at all like one of those times when you check out a guy and he looks away and then he checks you out and you look away. NO, he WANTED me to see his eyes connect with mine. When the hostess sat he and his friends across from us, he -of course- picked the seat that faced me directly. He smiled at me in such a way that all of my girlfriends were blushing for me. I was definitely envied that night; he was terribly handsome. But I challenged him, and kept my cool. I stared right back at him as if to say, "I am not, at all, intimidated by your looks! I am a... sensual, beautiful... intelligent woman. YOU should be intimidated by ME!! HAH! Then I got up in my slinky, sexy dress and walked like a superstar towards the bathroom. He of course followed... (*she jumps up and down excited*) and then, just outside the coat check room, I felt him touch my hair and my shoulder. I quickly turned around angry... and excited, (*with a full Covergirl spin and hair flip*) "Excuse me!"

HE says, "I am so sorry, but you are absolutely the most beautiful girl I have ever seen… are you single?" I nod for a long time and finally say, "Yes." I smiled, he smiled, and we stared into each other's eyes for a long time.

"Can I kiss you?" he moved my hair away from my face. Then… without looking away… but instead looking deeper into him I said it:

"I have a little girl, she is three." And then I watched …as this handsome, aggressive, ladies man let the thought of a three year old little girl turn his stare to the floor and his superhero aura into a terrified little lamb. Then I took his little lamb arm and told him that he could go back to his table now. He looked at me and then walked away… slowly. When I got back to my friends he and his whole table had already left. Oh… and he had also paid our tab. That night I held my little girl extra tight, I knew she wasn't my anchor… no… she was my manFILTER!! And also… my first… true… love.

NOTES

NOTES

Socks

I had just finished bartending when Laura begged me to go to dinner with her, her new boyfriend, and his friend. They had been visiting me up at the martini bar and I had shaken them up quite a few martinis. Now I was really not interested in the boyfriend's friend, but I knew that Laura wanted some "alone time" with her new boyfriend Rick. Rick, I call him "Rick the Dick" because he is a real jerk off. He flirts with anything in a skirt especially when he is drunk. And well, he was LOADED on this particular evening, thanks to me. He insisted on taking us to some FRENCH restaurant uptown where he is a regular so he could show off. By the time we'd ordered, he had shifted his seat so close to mine that he was practically sitting on my lap. Oh... oh oh... and he's from London Loooonnnddddonnn... so every perverted thing he said was colored with an English accent. (*clearing her throat, and changing her body posture into that of a decrepit vulgar animal*)

"I know you're Laura's friend, but I find you terribly attractive. Why don't you and I slip off to the loo together, what do you say?" (*imitating him, she licks her chops disgustingly, then goes back to her normal posture*)

I guess he thought Laura had selective hearing or something, and she was trying real hard to keep up a smile. Now, since I had been bartending all day, I was wearing a low cut shirt, oh ummm... much like this one, and I had displayed myself quite nicely... oh ummm much like I have now. HOWEVER, not for Rick the Dick. For tips at the bar. Poor Rick thought it was all for him. I longed for a sweatshirt as he became more and more obnoxious. I could tell that Laura was getting really offended and hurt, and I was beginning to think it was all my fault. So, after the THIRD time he told Laura to leave the restaurant so he could persuade me to allow him to touch me, I decided to let him in on a little secret. And so, I shook for him (*she shakes*) and I pouted for him, (*she pouts ridiculously over sexy*) and I leaned in real close... until I thought Laura might kill me. And then I let him have it.

(SHE PULLS OUT SEVEREL ENOURMOUS SOCKS OUT OF HER BRA REVEALING SHE IS NOT BUSTY AT ALL)

"THIS (*the socks in her hands*) is what's controlling your behavior, you moron!"

And you know what? I do believe I cured him. He became so shocked, he knocked his cosmopolitan into his filet mignon. Laura went into a laughing frenzy and his friend starting doing a puppet show with my socks. All in all, I'd say it was a very productive evening, (*with an British accent*) "INDEED."

NOTES

NOTES

Wonder Woman

Don't do this to me right now! Do you have any idea how difficult this job is? You knew who I was when you married me Tyrone!! I do not have time for this right now!! There are at least three hundred people drowning in seven different states, and at least sixty-seven accidents about to happen within just this state right now, at this very moment! What am I suppose to tell them? Huh? (*bending down on one knee*) "I am so sorry little girl, but my husband was feeling a little neglected this afternoon so I needed to rub his belly and most importantly his ego.?!" Supergirl is fed up with picking up the slack and keeps saying, "Bitch, that's what you get for breaking up with my cousin superman, and marrying a HUMAN of all things."

I am having a hard time making up excuses for our marital problems. Now come on honey… SNAP OUT OF IT! I love you!! I have loved you ever since the day I rescued you from that baby raccoon! Ummm, I'm sorry the "ATTACKING" baby raccoon. You looked so adorable there, screaming like a little girl in the middle of central park, at your office picnic. (*Sighs*) You must believe me the thing with Spidey was over before I even met you and, quite frankly, the only reason why it lasted as long as it did was because he was so damn flexible! Hmmmm BUT... BUT you... you are so vulnerable and sensitive I absolutely adore you. Now honey, you know I love my job! Don't you know that? It is hard, but I am good at it... damn good... so good, that people still think that Wonder Women IS WHITE! Now listen!! I will be picking you up tonight at your office on the eighty-seventh floor. I want you to leave the window open, I will pick you up in the invisible jet. We will completely avoid rush hour and have a lovely romantic dinner and then, after dinner, (*smiling wickedly*) I'm gonna' show you, just how wonderful... this Wonder Woman can be.

NOTES

NOTES

Orgasm Man

I love it when my girlfriend has an orgasm! Especially when I have caused it. It makes me feel like I have special powers... ya know... like a superhero! (*his eyes light up*) "ORGASM MAN"

Yeah... Yeah! Whenever women hear that I am coming into town they all run and get their hair done all giggling and excited, (*girlie voice*) "ORGASM MAN IS COMING!!! ORGASM MAN IS COMING!!"

I will go from house to house SAVING women from their mundane sex lives... and their husbands don't even mind! When I come to the door, (*ringing the bell with his groin area*) ding dong... the husband is watching his football... he turns to me and says, "HELLO ORGASM MAN, thank oh thank you, thank you (*on his knees*) thank you for coming! Wife's upstairs, say... can you throw me a beer on your way up?"

No but seriously it is just that you women are so beautiful and it really is sooo satisfying to give you so much pleasure. You women deserve it for putting up with all of our bullshit! It is the least we can do!

(*a voice from offstage*) HONEY ARE YOU COMING BACK TO BED?

(*BIG SMILE*) Well citizens… there is work to be done!

NOTES

NOTES

Expensive

I have been a whore, gigolo, prostitute, whatever you want to call it for so long it seems to be the only thing that I have ever been good at. My first client was one of my mother's friends. My mother was having a big dinner party. I was fourteen and Mrs. McKenzie, our pastor's wife, asked me if I would go downstairs with her to the wine cellar. She said she needed some help from a strong, young, man. As soon as we reached the bottom of the stairs, she grabbed my little ass like she wanted to take a piece home with her. Then she ripped open my trousers and climbed on top of me. When she was done, she threw me fifty quid and went back upstairs. I was overwhelmed. Not only had I just experienced my first sexual encounter with an actual live woman, but also I was practically rich. But I couldn't help but feel a little guilty. I mean after all, this was our pastors wife, right? I finally summoned up the courage to tell my mother what had happened. When I told her, she smacked me across the face and said, "How dare you say such things about the McKenzie's!!! They are servants of God, don't you ever make up such filthy lies like that again!" So every Sunday Mrs. McKenzie would find an excuse to take me away from Church, while Mr. McKenzie was in the midst of a sermon. She did things to me that I had only seen in magazines. By the time I got to high school, I was a real pro and expected a lot more than I was getting from the high school girls. So I started dating older women. First the university girls and then my professors and even eventually my friends mothers. I lost a lot of friends. It was as if I was this older woman magnet. Like they just knew I was trained properly or something. Oh yeah, and they all paid me. Not always money. For example, my French teacher gave me my most outstanding grades and I don't even know how to say "It's a beautiful day" in French. But all the others paid me and I quit school and was able to start my own service through referrals. I am now twenty-six and have been with hundreds of women. And I know how to please every one of them. You know why? Because I understand that every single one is different. Like a flower, or a star, or a butterfly. When they step into my house I can tell in the first five minutes what it is they long for. Have I ever been in love? Well now… that all depends on how much is in your wallet.

NOTES

NOTES

Whenever

I still become so weak at the mere sight of you. I see you crossing the street towards me and my whole being lights up. I can't help but smile. I have someone new to love and be loved by. He loves me respectfully like you never did... But I still have hope when I see you smile at me. I long for you to hear my jokes and tell me yours. I wish to know how you spend your days and who you pass by on the street. I miss seeing your responses to some silly advertisement and your excitement over some baseball game. I wonder if you still eat everything on everyone's plate with other girls. Or if you've changed your ways because of them. How are you trying to impress people? Who did you make angry? Who is glad they just met you? Do you still sleep hugging the pillow and arise in a panic always assuming that you are running late. Do you still make love like a [...] with others? I'll never know. I can't afford to love you. But I still wonder whenever you smile at me.

NOTES

Complimentary

This may sound crazy to you, but even though I'm a guy, I really DON'T want to sleep with every girl know or meet. For some reason, this very fact makes you women want to sleep with me even MORE! What is it with you women? You only want something when you can't have it and man are you manipulative!! I've heard it all:

"COME ON OVER… ITS JUST SEX…"

"IT WON'T CHANGE A THING BETWEEN US!"

"NO STRINGS ATTACHED"

"IT'S JUST AN INDOOR SPORT!"

"I'M LONELY THAT'S ALL"

"YOU'RE THE ONLY GUY I TRUST TO HAVE CASUAL SEX WITH!"

"YOURE JUST SOOOOOOO HOTTTTTTT"

"WON'T IT BE SOOO GREAT THINK ABOUT IT!!!"

"FINE, HOW ABOUT JUST ORAL SEX THEN !!"

You get me all hot and bothered about what you're gonna' do to my this and what you're gonna' do to my that. It becomes this ultimate challenge between your dirty sexual advances, and my sudden indecisiveness between right and wrong, and why would I ever turn down casual sex to begin with, questioning my very manhood, wondering how I ever managed to get myself in this situation! But then... just as I am about to surrender like Adam to Eve, I become incredibly repulsed by your desperation and leave. Then because of this I am now a dick, a loser insensitive, insulting, I've bruised your ego and now you hate me. I thought only moments ago I was "the only guy you could trust?" When you turn down a woman when she's offering herself to you completely, boy does she become enraged!!! It's a scary thing! But sometimes ladies we just want to be friends. I know it may seem like most men are ruled by their penis, but that does not mean that you should try to take advantage of us. Besides, there are a few of us left who still have some self control and will do the right thing no matter how alluring you can be, yes, that's right! Sooo... Jezebel... That is your name right? Why am I telling you this? I am telling you all of this because I really feel that to compensate for all women, I really deserve for this next lap dance to be complimentary.

NOTES

NOTES

My MUSIC

Now, as a musician, I get more than my fair share of the ladies. Almost every night I play, no matter what club it is, there is always at least one woman standing around, watching me... mesmerized by my raw talent. As soon as I spot her out, I motion the waiter to refresh her drink. I already know that she is the little lady I will be serenading all night. (*plays a little*) and she smiles at me, (*plays a little more*) and her dress slips to the floor. (*Laughing*) And I know I am not wasting my time because my notes and melodies that are floating in the air have lured her to me and she is under my spell... because she can hear and feel, and sense my rhythms like a preview of what her night could possibly bring to her. The only problem I have is... well, loving my music just a little more than my ladies. That may have cost me what people call... "true love." But you know what, maybe one day I will meet that woman who will put ME under HER spell. Who knows, maybe you could be her... what are you doing tonight baby girl? (*Plays more and walks away to back out.*)

NOTES

Dirty Sheets

So he called me two days in a row, asking me to come over. He said he "missed" me a lot and that he really wanted to see me. I said, "No." My instincts knew it wasn't a good idea. He had decided recently that he wanted to date other people, to ensure that I was really "the One," especially since I'm seven years older than he is. However, the next day was Friday, and I was throwing my usual Friday night party at the Imperial York Restaurant. I'm a promoter there once a week. And a lot of people weren't showing, so I called him to see if maybe he could bring some people, since we had decided to be friends. Well he was rude to me, and incredibly short. And I asked him was he working and he said "Yes" and that he had to go. I immediately felt like I had fallen, even though I was still standing. I knew something was up. He was with a girl, and there really wasn't anything I could do about it, because he told me he wanted to see other people. I became mildly enraged, but still had to be a lovely host to my guests. So at one AM, I called him again, from someone else's cell phone. And he answered, and he was still rude. So I asked him, "Are you on a date?" And he said

"Yes." I hung up immediately and began to freak -internally. And before I could let anybody see, I asked this girl Aileen, who I had just met, if she would come downstairs to the ladies room with me. I could tell she was a cool chick. I could see it in her face. So I cried and complained to my new friend, and I told her I really wanted to go over there. I wanted to see him in action with this girl. And, of course, most importantly I wanted to see what she looked like. Well Aileen convinced me not to. So I went home and called him a few hundred times. And the phone just kept ringing. No answering machine. He had turned the ringer off. That meant he was fucking her. I began burning with rage that only Medea could truly understand. I decided I had to go over there, and I would in the morning. So at eight AM, I got up and headed over there, shaking and feeling mildly electric. I went straight past the doormen, who know me and love me, because I've been coming there for three years. I rang the bell three times and hid on the side, so he wouldn't know it was me, in case he wouldn't answer, which is already crazy, because supposedly he loves me still. Anyway, soon he answers, and he's half asleep, in his boxers. "You can't come in," he says. Actually, now that I think about it, he just says, "No!" and shakes his head like an idiot. So I sweetly say, "Oh, I just need my black Bebe dress. I'll wait right here." And I smile at him innocently, with my lips closed. He heads toward the closet in his room, and two seconds later, I'm right behind him, still hoping to see our bed in his room empty. Of course it isn't. I see her. She has long hair, and she's not that pretty, although I wish now that I had gotten a better look. And she sees me, and just ... turns over. She is naked. And I wanted to scream: "You don't belong here. Your naked body is infecting my sheets, you fucking whore." But I don't. Steve grabs my arm to throw me out, and I stop in the hallway to grab my curling iron, and I say, "She's ugly." He gets mad and says, "Get out now!" and tries to push me out, as I avoid the door, take a detour into the living room, and sit down on the couch. "Why are you doing this?" I ask him. He pretends that he's calling the police on me. I say, "Turn the light on. I want you to see me." He says, "Well, I guess this is how it has to be now?" As if there were another choice. And I say, "No, Steve, this is how it is. You just asked me over yesterday." "No I didn't!" he says ridiculously loud in case the whore can hear me. "Oh really, Steve? You didn't just say, 'Please come over. We're going the same direction in the morning'?" He says nothing, and I can't believe he's protecting her, and hurting me. He's also lying to ensure that she'll still like him. He has become a creep. And that hurts more than the ugly slut who's sleeping without concern on my sheets.

NOTES

Notes You Can Use or Not

Bulgarian Princess:

The word SWALLOW is important

Sarcasm works here and there but there is definitely a time to be serious

Blue Light Special:

"It was just soooo...(really search for what it "was") before saying ugly

Watch him walk away and make sure he really leaves, the truth is that he can come back and do "anything" to you

Wonder Woman:

She must be African American

"She" can be a "He" though if desired, also fabulous drag queens are always welcome

Weening:

Done best if done totally straight meaning

Bon Appetite:

Can be done by either gender and you can obviously change Chinese Food to any cuisine desired that works for actor's ethnicity etc.

Promise:

Difficult to get out at first and then it pours out

She Can't Be Trusted:

Best done Italian Brooklyn, Bronx style but have had thick Russian accent work as well.

He is truly damaged by his mother

Perhaps, not the sharpest tool.

Believes one day she's going to wake up see through his eyes ... a severely wounded, but killer, dog.

Someone:

A pillow helps

She is in her hospital room

Fearless:

Have fun reliving the short romantic encounter; take your time with every sexy move

He is ridiculously hot ...on the outside

Friendly Fire:

Make sure you know what" friendly fire" means

She absolutely owns you

She is luscious

I Can't Get No:

Works nicely when begun angelic. So incredibly frustrating and unfair.

Socks:

A bra with a different color...usually pink or red from the dress or top you are wearing also helps to draw attention innocently to your "chest area"

Make sure the socks are ready to go! But not seen until the end of course!

Can be done with Brooklyn or southern accent...but way over the top with the British accent and replaying RICK like a dirty beast licking his chops manner ...body too

Complimentary:

Each girl you reenact has a very different persuasiveness they all must be different and specific in your memory even though they have the same goal

You are nothing but a victim and need to stand up for mankind

You #1:

A beat after the first "I" before "Love you"

Syrup – Like, with Lots of energy

Every time you say "you" Whoever "you" is ... MUST be seen clearly by actor, we must see him in your eyes

Stars in your eyes

You #2:

A beat after the first "I" before "hate you"

Use the "T" sound in hate

Builds momentum big time ...spewing

Daggers in your eyes

Sumi's Hands:

Done with any Asian accent matching of course where character is from

Beat before and after "I miss her sex"

Expensive:

Beat before "Whore" in the beginning

There can be people sleeping on a bed behind him whoever those people are, says a lot about what kind of "services" he does.

So Bored With You:

"I Feel Like ..." discover slowly what you feel like and each idea gets you more and more excited when you think of laughing on the beach... LAUGH enjoy it ... show us your neck, your face, your lips... sexy energy until "Someone else, not you". Take your time nice and slooow

My Mission:

Just trying to find the right key, to get inside. Ego stimulates him to keep trying. Enjoy moment of last try that works. Prepare yourself in a delicious way.

Morning Sun:

He truly believes he is in love, probably in his jail cell, or holding cell still cuffed.

THANK YOU

Florence Arqueros, Carolyn Campisi, Nick Read, Daniel, Bobbie and Dustin Read, Terry Dancik, Beth, Carmine and Donovan Arqueros, Jane Blomquist, Wesley Abbott, Ann Horton, Sheryl Guterman, Aaron Jettleson, Tori Amos, Mickie Freidman, Michelle Justick, Ally, Spalding Gray, Lavonne and Kathryn J. Myrick, Jason Kyle Pepper, Julio Martinez, LuLu Wilson, Lavinia Arriaza, Mahira Amir Khan, Derek Jeter, Sarah Moore, Fran Drescher, Brian, Henry and Laura Daley, Michael Beckett, Linda Guess, Sarah Jones, John Waters, Steve and Amy Kurland, Paul Harmon, Candita Mamet, Michelle Santopietro, Barry Manilow, Dr. Lerrick, John and Ed Priddy, David Remfry, Vincent Perez, Percy Leon, Nancy Jeanne, Chuck Zito, Joe and Harry Gantz, The Superheroes from Hollywood Blvd., Corby Ann Stutzman, Jessica Sheese, James Lee, Jeff Keil, Anne and X Tejada, David Markell, Colonel Bernard and Mrs. Linda Wray, Bob De Groff, Venus, Samson, Advil, and Willow.

In increasingly day-to-day loving memory of
Uncle Bernie, Laura Daley, and Dustin Read.

*– and a shout out to Miguel Piñero
and the Lower east side*

I feel Piñero and his lower east side drive
I understand without calculating why
I just understand
Comprehend
The world he mends

I was born and raised in Hollywood without a star
My momma without a car

Sitting at the bus stops
Stared at by the horny pops
        By the horny cops

Believing they could give me the ride I needed
Still excited 'til I was heated
By their friendly faces retreated,
Back, way back
Wanting my body, wanting my soul
I just needed a ride
But didn't want to pay that toll
This isn't the destination I intended
This isn't the grown up I befriended

Yet, like a good little girl
I paid,
They got laid
Just another little girl frayed
And Now I ain't mad,
I'm not even jaded
Still love men without even hatin'
If they can be wolves
Well then, I can be Satan

My hair was yellow and my skin was white
But that didn't light up those Hollywood nights
I was also half Latina because of my father's blood and sperm

Who is he?
Where is he?
Will I ever see his face?

Do I have his eyes?

Could he have protected?
Given me some perspective?
Or is he just another fool arrested?

Well,... I hear I have 5 brothers.

I'm a grown woman now,
But I still carry that time,
Like a clock tic tocking in my mind
as my love takes me from behind...

I STRIVE TO BE KIND.

Joelle

Printed in the United States
134616LV00003B/6/P